— Discovering Canada —
Roald Amundsen

Weigl
CALGARY
www.weigl.com

Leia Tait

Published by Weigl Educational Publishers Limited
6325 10 Street SE
Calgary, Alberta, Canada
T2H 2Z9

Website: www.weigl.com
Copyright ©2009 Weigl Educational Publishers Limited
All rights reserved. No part of this publication may be reproduced, stored in a retrieval system, or transmitted in any form or by any means, electronic, mechanical, photocopying, recording, or otherwise, without the prior written permission of the publisher.

All of the Internet URLs given in the book were valid at the time of publication. However, due to the dynamic nature of the Internet, some addresses may have changed, or sites may have ceased to exist since publication. While the author and publisher regret any inconvenience this may cause readers, no responsibility for any such changes can be accepted by either the author or the publisher.

Library and Archives Canada Cataloguing in Publication data available upon request.
Fax (403) 233-7769 for the attention of the Publishing Records department.

ISBN 978-1-55388-500-7 (hard cover)
ISBN 978-1-55388-501-5 (soft cover)

Printed in the United States of America
1 2 3 4 5 6 7 8 9 0   12 11 10 09 08

We acknowledge the financial support of the Government of Canada through the Book Publishing Industry Development Program (BPIDP) for our publishing activities.

PROJECT COORDINATOR
Heather C. Hudak

DESIGN
Terry Paulhus

CREDITS: Every reasonable effort has been made to trace ownership and to obtain permission to reprint copyright material. The publishers would be pleased to have any errors or omissions brought to their attention so that they may be corrected in subsequent printings.

Photograph credits: Weigl acknowledges Getty Images as the primary image supplier for this title.

Other photograph credits include: Dreamstime: pages 11, 29; Alamy: pages 18, 20, 22; Phil Conroy: page 16.

CONTENTS

Introduction 4
Early Years 6
Amundsen's Ventures 8

Exploring for Riches 10
Ships and Tools 12
Polar Preparation 14

Into the Arctic 16
Safe Passage 18
Out of the Cold 20

Surviving the Arctic 22
Lasting Achievements and Legacies 24
Explorer Expeditions 26

Timeline 28
Create a Compass 29
Quiz 30

Websites/Books 31
Glossary/Index 32

Introduction

In the early 1900s, Roald Amundsen was a polar explorer. From childhood, it was his dream to explore the Arctic. He struggled to raise money for his first voyage in 1903, but quickly overcame many challenges. In fact, Amundsen was one of the most successful polar explorers ever, making important discoveries in both the Arctic and the Antarctic. He found routes other explorers had been seeking for centuries, and travelled to places on Earth no one else had ever been.

Explorer Essentials

Amundsen took part in nearly every significant polar exploration achievement that happened during his lifetime.

Curiosity about wealth and need for simplified trade routes drove European explorers to sail across the ocean.

985 Norse explorers travel to northeast parts of the Canadian Arctic.

4

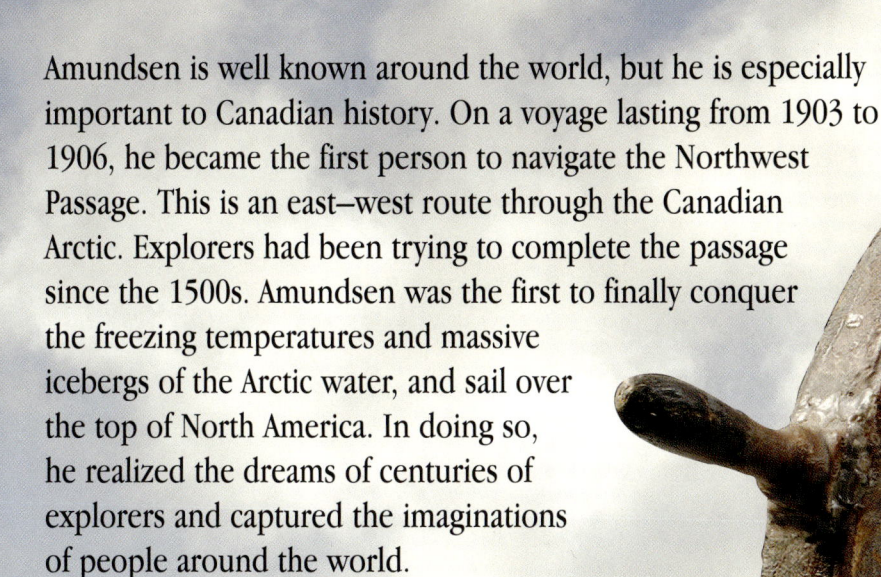

Amundsen is well known around the world, but he is especially important to Canadian history. On a voyage lasting from 1903 to 1906, he became the first person to navigate the Northwest Passage. This is an east–west route through the Canadian Arctic. Explorers had been trying to complete the passage since the 1500s. Amundsen was the first to finally conquer the freezing temperatures and massive icebergs of the Arctic water, and sail over the top of North America. In doing so, he realized the dreams of centuries of explorers and captured the imaginations of people around the world.

- Early explorers used wooden ships that relied on manual steering and sails. By Amundsen's lifetime, engines and other technology were being used to improve ships' abilities.

1497 John Cabot explores Canada's east coast in search of a seaway to Asia. He finds no passage, but claims the land for King Henry VII of England.

1535 Hoping he has found a route to Asia, French explorer Jacques Cartier is the first European to sail the St. Lawrence River in what is now Quebec.

1576 On several trips to the Canadian Arctic, Martin Frobisher explores Baffin Island, the coast of Labrador, and the islands of present-day Nunavut.

1610 Henry Hudson discovers Hudson Bay. His crew sets him adrift in the bay after enduring many hardships in their quest for the Northwest Passage.

1845 John Franklin and his entire crew perish on his third attempt to find the Northwest Passage.

Early Years

On July 16, 1872, Roald Engebreth Gravning Amundsen was born. He lived with his parents and three older brothers in Borge. This is a town near Oslo, the capital city of Norway.

As a boy, Amundsen enjoyed reading about the adventures of well-known explorers. One day, Amundsen read about John Franklin, a British polar explorer from the mid-1800s. Franklin survived many hardships in the Canadian Arctic before disappearing on a voyage to discover the Northwest Passage. Amundsen was impressed by Franklin's skill and courage. He was also fascinated by the ongoing search for the Northwest Passage. Amundsen decided that he would become a polar explorer. Finding the Northwest Passage became his dream.

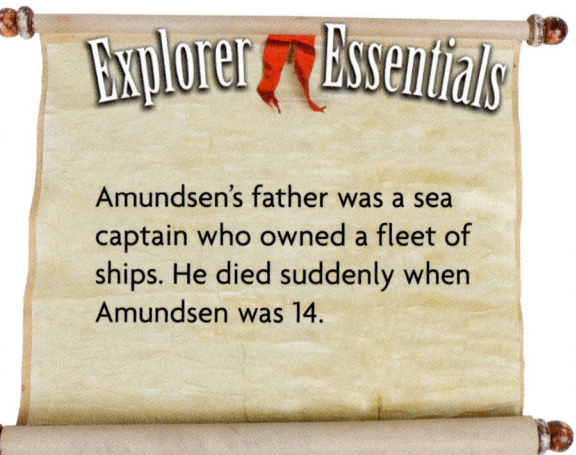

Explorer Essentials

Amundsen's father was a sea captain who owned a fleet of ships. He died suddenly when Amundsen was 14.

- Oslo was founded in roughly 1000 AD. It has been the capital of Norway since 1814, when Norway gained its independence from Denmark.

Amundsen began preparing for his future career. He read every book he could find about polar exploration. To condition his body to cold, he slept with his bedroom window open on winter nights. He also hiked long distances in the mountains around Oslo. These hikes strengthened his muscles and taught him how to move on ice and snow.

Amundsen completed school when he was 18 and joined the Norwegian army. He believed army life would be ideal training for his future as an explorer. However, Amundsen's mother urged him to become a doctor, so he left the army and studied medicine for a short time. When his mother died in 1893, Amundsen quit medical school. He was more determined than ever to become a polar explorer.

- Franklin made four journeys to the Arctic. On his second journey, he and the crew ran out of food and were forced to eat the leather parts on their clothing.

The Franklin Expeditions

Sir John Franklin (1786–1847) made three voyages to Arctic Canada in search of the Northwest Passage. During his first voyage in 1819, nine of his crew died from extreme cold and hunger. In 1827, Franklin returned to explore more than 1,500 kilometres of coast in what is now the Northwest Territories. Twenty years later, Franklin's third voyage met a tragic end. In 1847, his two ships became trapped in ice near King William Island. Franklin and 23 members of his crew died waiting for the ice to melt. The others perished trying to walk to the Bock River in present-day Nunavut. Their fate was not discovered until 1857, when handwritten notes were found inside a rock **cairn**. In the meantime, dozens of ships searched the Canadian Arctic for the missing sailors. These explorations opened up the area for future explorers, including Amundsen. Today, Franklin is remembered as a hero.

Amundsen's Ventures

To learn more about sailing in northern waters, Amundsen took a job onboard a **sealing** vessel. He worked hard, and in 1897, became **first mate** of a ship called the *Belgica*. The ship was bound for Antarctica on a mission to explore the coast. It was Amundsen's first true polar expedition. When the *Belgica* reached Antarctica in January 1898, Amundsen and the rest of the crew mapped the area now known as Gerlache Strait.

The *Belgica* was set to return to Europe at the end of February. On the last day of the month, sea ice formed around the ship, trapping it in place. As a result, Amundsen and the crew accidentally became the first people to spend the winter in Antarctica.

The *Belgica*'s crew were not prepared for an Antarctic winter. They soon became ill from the cold and lack of fresh food. When the captain's health grew worse, Amundsen took control. Under his leadership, the *Belgica* finally broke free of the ice in March 1899 and headed home to Europe. Afterwards, Amundsen always remembered the lessons he learned on that voyage, especially the value of careful planning.

- To keep the *Belgica* crew from starving, Amundsen urged them to hunt seals and penguins. He also had the ship's store of blankets sewn into suits to help keep the crew warm.

Antarctica

Antarctica is the fifth-largest continent in the world. It is surrounded by rough seas that kept explorers away until 1820. Colder than the Arctic, Antarctica is almost entirely covered by a thick sheet of ice. It is home to some plants and animals, including fur seals, penguins, and sea birds. The Antarctic summer lasts from September to March. During this time, the Sun never sets. This is followed by six months of dark winter. Then, a thick belt of sea ice forms around the coast.

Exploring for Riches

Since the late 1400s, Europeans had been seeking the Northwest Passage in order to reach Asia. They wanted easier access to the silks, spices, and other precious goods available there. By 1900, the route still had not been found. It was clear that even if it existed, the Northwest Passage would not be useful for trade. Only the most devoted explorers still continued to look for it. Inspired by Franklin, Amundsen decided to begin his own search. He hoped that, with careful planning and determination, he could discover the route that had eluded others for so long.

Explorer Essentials

In preparation for his voyage to the Arctic, Amundsen earned his ship captain's license in 1900.

First, Amundsen needed money. Polar exploration was costly, and few investors were interested in finding the Northwest Passage. Instead, they were funding expeditions that could lead to important scientific discoveries.

Amundsen knew his voyage needed a scientific purpose. He decided to search for the current location of the North Magnetic Pole. Explorer James Clark Ross had first located the pole in 1831 on the west coast of Boothia Peninsula, which is a large peninsula in the Canadian Arctic. However, scientists and sailors both believed the pole had moved since then. Amundsen decided to find out for certain. He would travel to the Canadian Arctic to gather scientific data about the pole. Then, he would search for the Northwest Passage.

■ An early form of the compass, in which a magnetized needle floated in water, was invented in China some time before 1044 AD.

The North Magnetic Pole

When the first compasses were invented, people believed their needles pointed to a magnetic mountain in the North. By the 1400s, sailors realized their compasses did not point directly north. Instead, they pointed to a mark that was slightly off true north. This point is called the North Magnetic Pole. It is one of two places on Earth where the planet's natural magnetic force is strongest. The North Magnetic Pole is different from the North Pole, which is true north.

11

Ships and Tools

With his purpose decided, Amundsen began preparing for the voyage. First, he went to the Hamburg Maritime Institute in Germany. There, he spent six weeks studying **geomagnetism**. He learned how to measure and record information about Earth's magnetic forces and how to locate the North Magnetic Pole.

Next, Amundsen needed a ship. In 1900, he purchased a small, single-masted fishing boat called the *Gjøa*. It was 21 metres long and 6.5 metres wide. Some people thought the *Gjøa* was too small to survive battering by the Arctic's massive icebergs, but Amundsen knew the boat's small size made it light and fast. Rather than forcing his way through the ice like many previous explorers, Amundsen planned to ease the *Gjøa* around the ice and through narrow waterways in an effort to find the Northwest Passage. To make the *Gjøa* more seaworthy, Amundsen reinforced its **hull** with thick oak and added iron strapping to the **bow**. He also outfitted it with a 13-horsepower diesel engine for increased **manoeuverability**.

■ Amundsen was born in Norway in 1872, the same year the *Gjøa* was built.

Finally, Amundsen gathered a crew. Each member would help sail the *Gjøa* and carry out special scientific duties. Helmer Hanssen was an experienced sailor. Anton Lund was a sealing skipper. Peder Ristvedt had been Amundsen's sergeant in the Norwegian army. He trained in **meteorology** for the expedition. Godred Hanson was a lieutenant in the Danish navy. Gustav Wiik, also a member of the Norwegian navy, would carry out magnetic measurements. Amundsen was the ship's captain. He would make important decisions and lead the expedition.

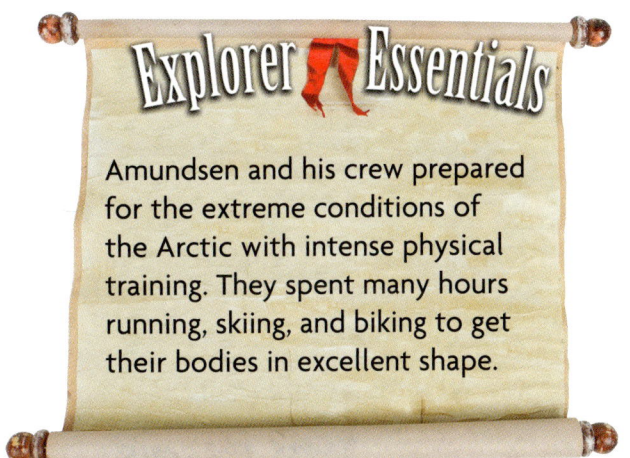

Explorer Essentials

Amundsen and his crew prepared for the extreme conditions of the Arctic with intense physical training. They spent many hours running, skiing, and biking to get their bodies in excellent shape.

First-Hand Account

In his autobiography, Amundsen described the many preparations he made for his expedition to the Canadian Arctic.

"In 1900, I bought the ship for this, my first expedition. She was a small fishing smack from the northern part of Norway. She was 47 tons and of the same age as myself… The winter and spring of 1902–1903 I spent in feverish preparation for my great adventure of the Northwest Passage. I besieged every possible source of funds—the learned societies and the private patrons of science. The rest of my time was spent in selecting and ordering supplies."

Polar Preparation

With his ship and crew ready, Amundsen began gathering supplies. First, he purchased equipment for magnetic research. He packed the instruments carefully in crates made with copper nails. This prevented ordinary steel nails from interfering with the magnetic readings. Amundsen also selected warm clothing for the entire crew and packed tents that could be used as temporary shelter on land.

For travel on land, Amundsen planned to use skis, as well as sleds pulled by dog teams. He spent time learning about sled dogs from Otto Sverdrup. Like Amundsen, Sverdrup was a Norwegian polar explorer. He had spent four years in the Canadian Arctic exploring Ellesmere Island. When he returned to Norway in 1902, Amundsen was on shore to greet him. Sverdrup told Amundsen all he knew about sledding. He even gave Amundsen a team of dogs.

Explorer Essentials

When nervous **creditors** threatened to seize the *Gjøa* before Amundsen's expedition had even begun, he and the crew secretly sailed out of Oslo at midnight on June 16, 1903.

- Amundsen was over 1.8 metres tall, and took pride in his nickname, "the last of the Vikings."

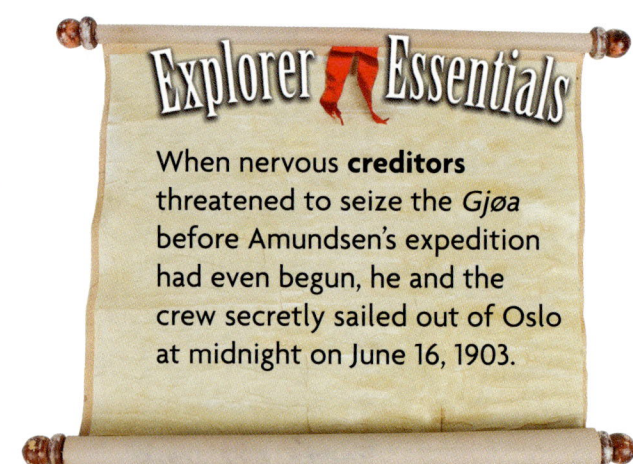

Amundsen also convinced Sverdrup's cook, Adolf Lindstrøm, to join his crew. The expedition was scheduled to last three years. Amundsen knew that having a good cook onboard would help keep the crew healthy and happy. They would have to rely on ingredients that would not easily spoil, such as coffee, powdered milk, wheat germ, biscuits, **pemmican**, and tinned fruits. Amundsen planned to supplement these with fresh meat from hunting and fishing. Above all, it was important that the food was nutritious. Having Lindstrøm onboard would help keep the crew from becoming ill with **scurvy**, which was common among polar explorers.

Finally, Amundsen and his crew were ready to embark on their journey. Even though they were packing light, the *Gjøa* barely stayed afloat once all the supplies were onboard.

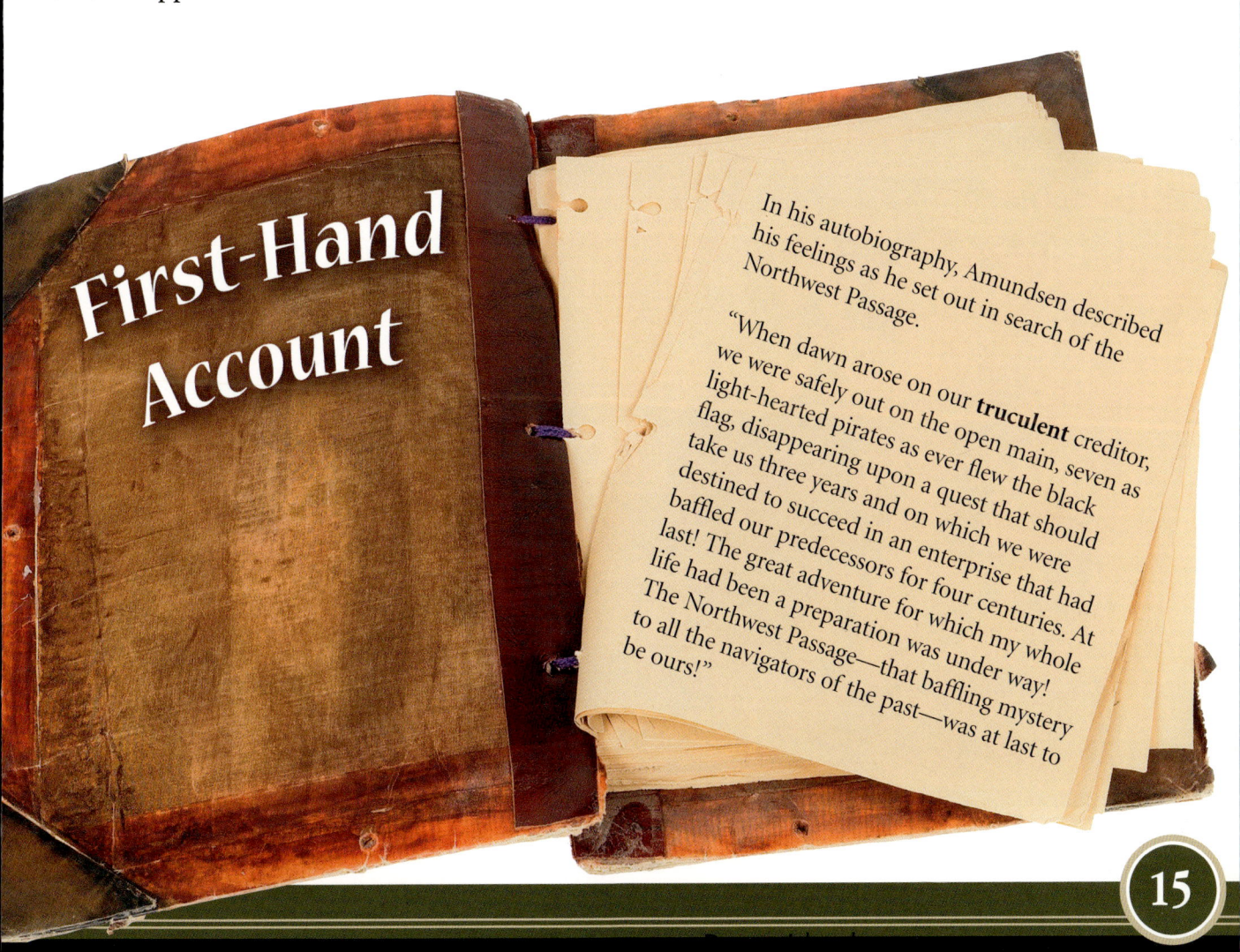

First-Hand Account

In his autobiography, Amundsen described his feelings as he set out in search of the Northwest Passage.

"When dawn arose on our **truculent** creditor, we were safely out on the open main, seven as light-hearted pirates as ever flew the black flag, disappearing upon a quest that should take us three years and on which we were destined to succeed in an enterprise that had baffled our predecessors for four centuries. At last! The great adventure for which my whole life had been a preparation was under way! The Northwest Passage—that baffling mystery to all the navigators of the past—was at last to be ours!"

Into the Arctic

From Norway, Amundsen and his crew sailed west across the Atlantic Ocean. They journeyed up Greenland's west coast, stopping to buy dog teams at Godhavn and supplies at Dalrymple Rock. Then, they headed west into **Lancaster Sound**. They stopped at Beechey Island in late August. There, Amundsen honoured his hero, Sir John Franklin, by visiting three graves belonging to members of Franklin's 1827 expedition.

The *Gjøa* then turned south into Peel Sound, east of Prince William Island. Shallow water, fog, and strong winds made travel here difficult. Twice, the *Gjøa* became stuck on rocks. The crew threw cases of dog food and other supplies overboard to lighten their load and help the ship sail over the rocks. Finally, in September 1903, they reached a small harbour on the southeast coast of King William Island. The harbour was sheltered and near the North Magnetic Pole. Amundsen thought it was an ideal spot to set up base camp. He named the place Gjøa Haven, and he and the crew went ashore.

■ Gjøa Haven is now a permanent Inuit community in Nunavut.

Amundsen's First Voyage 1903

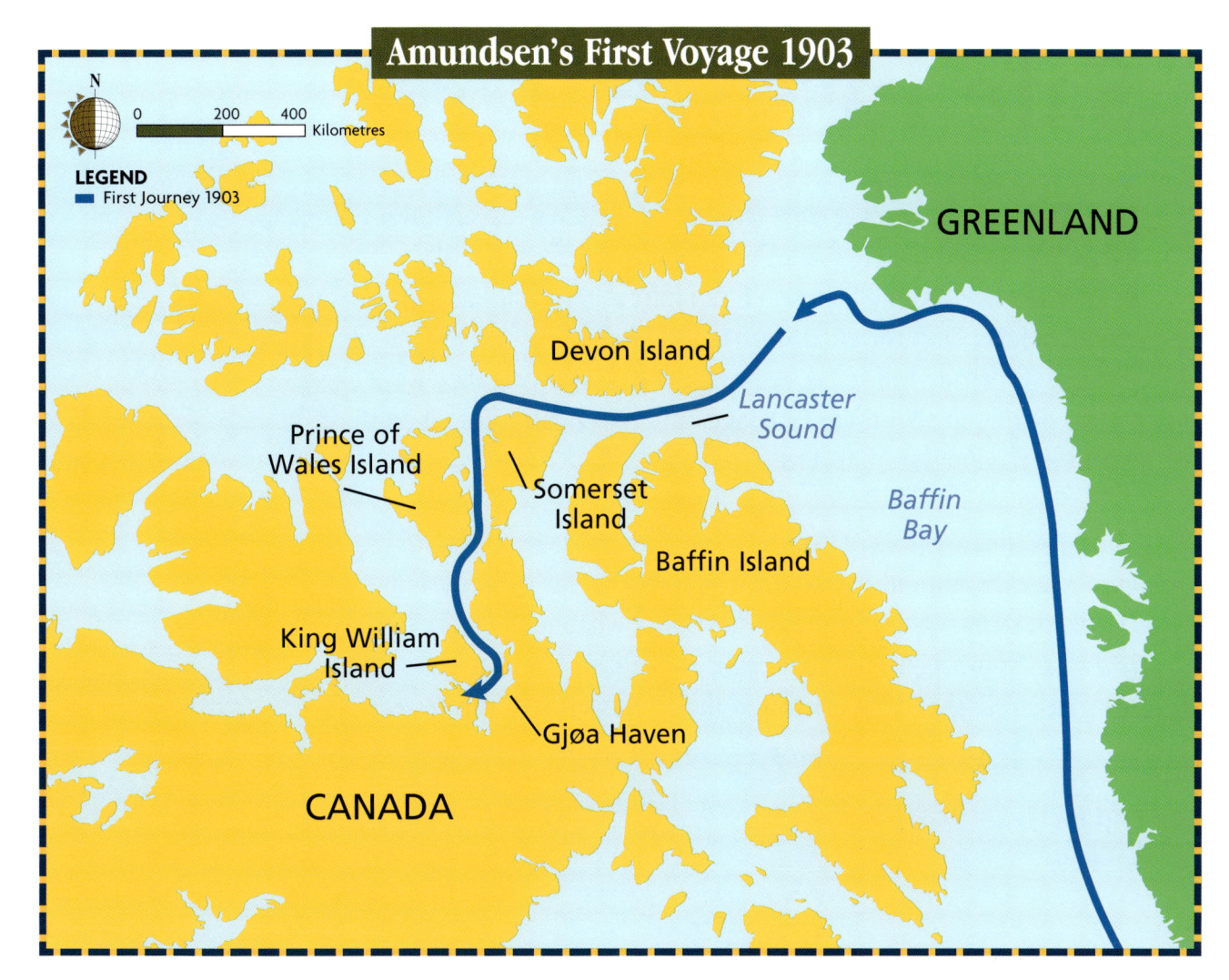

At Gjøa Haven, the crew built a house, shelters for their scientific equipment, and kennels for their sled dogs. They spent the next two years exploring the area and recording scientific data. Amundsen tried many times to reach the North Magnetic Pole. On April 26, 1904, he and Ristvedt reached Boothia Peninsula. Their equipment showed the pole had moved more than 60 kilometres northeast since Ross' discovery in 1831. Although Amundsen never reached the North Magnetic Pole, he proved that it moved. This helped scientists prove that Earth's core is not solid.

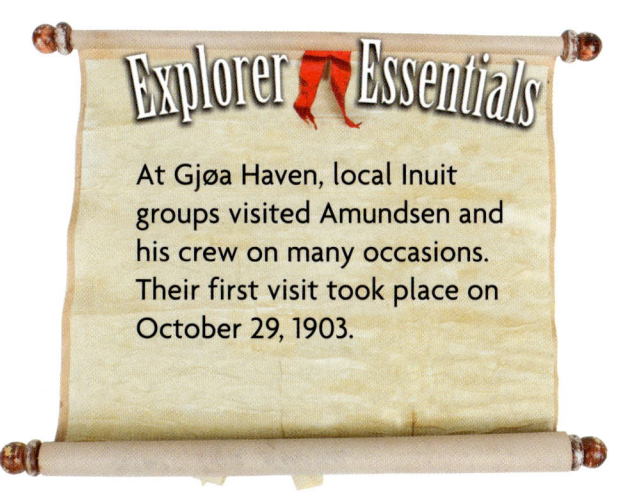

Explorer Essentials

At Gjøa Haven, local Inuit groups visited Amundsen and his crew on many occasions. Their first visit took place on October 29, 1903.

Safe Passage

After two years at Gjøa Haven, Amundsen's research was complete. He and the crew left the harbour on August 13, 1905. They sailed west through Simpson Strait into waters that had never been visited before. They travelled slowly, watching for ice, rocks, and other dangers. Everyone was tense with excitement, knowing they were close to completing the Northwest Passage. Amundsen later described these weeks as the longest of his life

The *Gjøa* finally emerged from waters south of Victoria Island. On August 26, Amundsen woke to the voices of his crew shouting, "Vessel in sight! Vessel in sight!" They saw a whaling ship, the *Charles Hansson*, approaching from the east. Amundsen wiped tears of joy from his eyes. They had completed the Northwest Passage.

- The first Inuit hunters that Amundsen met at Gjøa Haven had never smelled tobacco smoke. They thought Amundsen's pipe "smelled awful."

Amundsen's Second Voyage 1905–1906

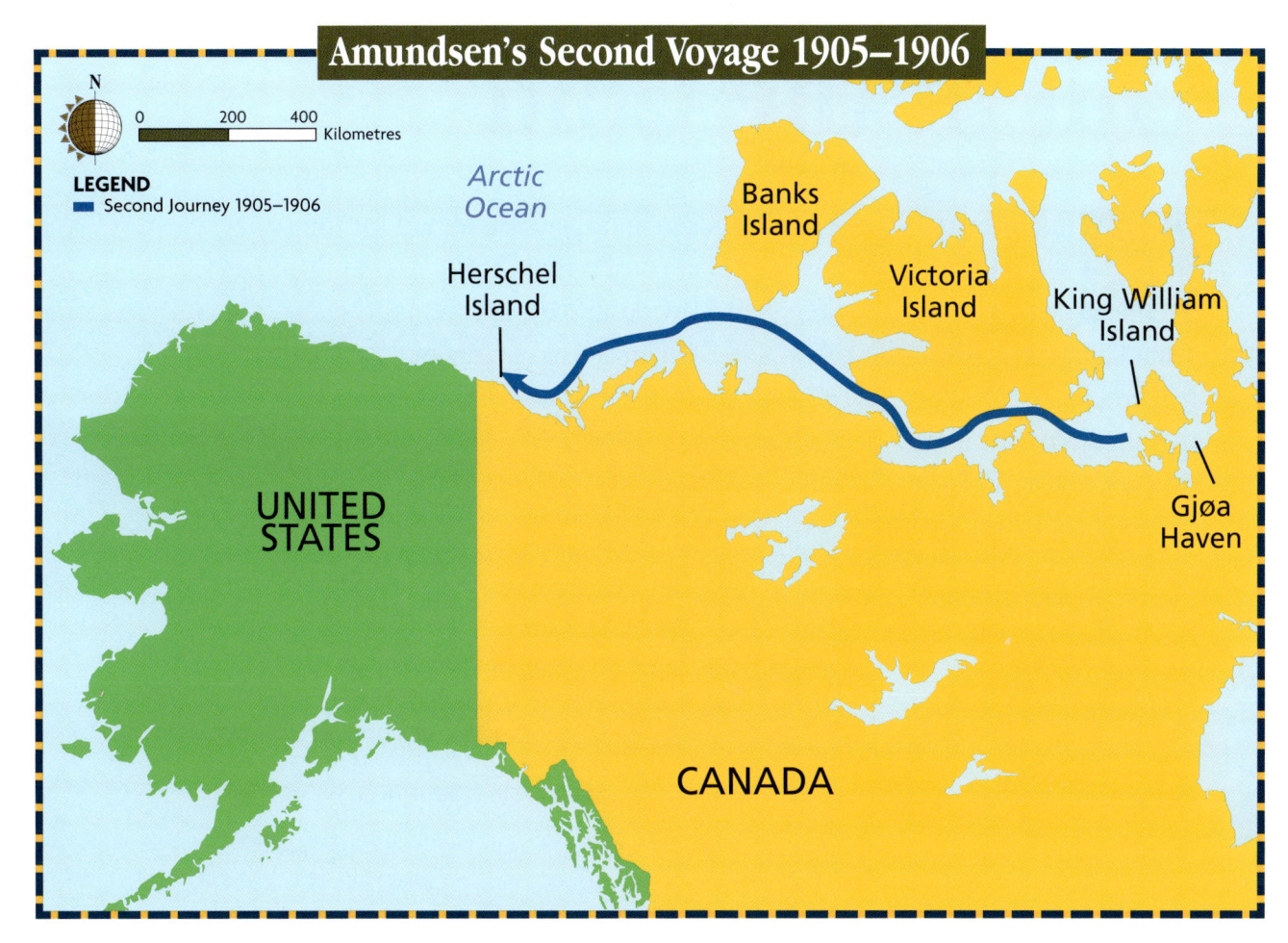

Within days, winter set in. The *Gjøa* became frozen in the Arctic ice off Herschel Island, near the Yukon coast. The crew had no choice but to spend another season in the Arctic.

Amundsen found it impossible to wait onboard. He wanted to share his news with the world. On October 24, he set out for Eagle City, Alaska. Travelling by dogsled and on skis, Amundsen crossed 800 kilometres of snow and ice, including the Brooks Mountain Range. He arrived in Eagle City on December 5. From nearby Fort Egbert, Amundsen sent a telegraph announcing his achievement to the world. Then, he returned through the ice and snow, reaching the *Gjøa* on March 12, 1906.

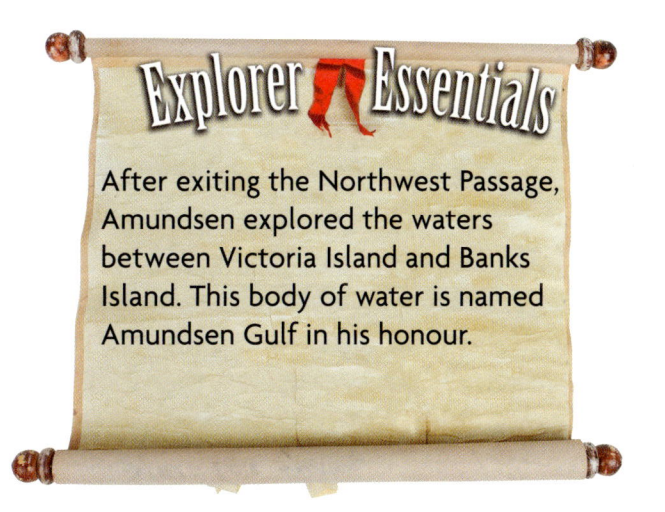

Explorer Essentials

After exiting the Northwest Passage, Amundsen explored the waters between Victoria Island and Banks Island. This body of water is named Amundsen Gulf in his honour.

Out of the Cold

Back onboard the *Gjøa*, Amundsen and the crew waited for the Arctic ice to melt. Gustav Wiik died of **appendicitis** during this time. In July, the others began working the *Gjøa* free of the ice. They sailed west, along the Yukon and Alaskan coasts. In August, the *Gjøa* reached Point Barrow, the northernmost point of Alaska. From there, the explorers turned southwest and then south, into the **Bering Strait**.

- Amundsen and the crew of the *Gjøa* arrived in San Francisco on October 16, 1903 to a hero's welcome.

Amundsen's Third Voyage 1906

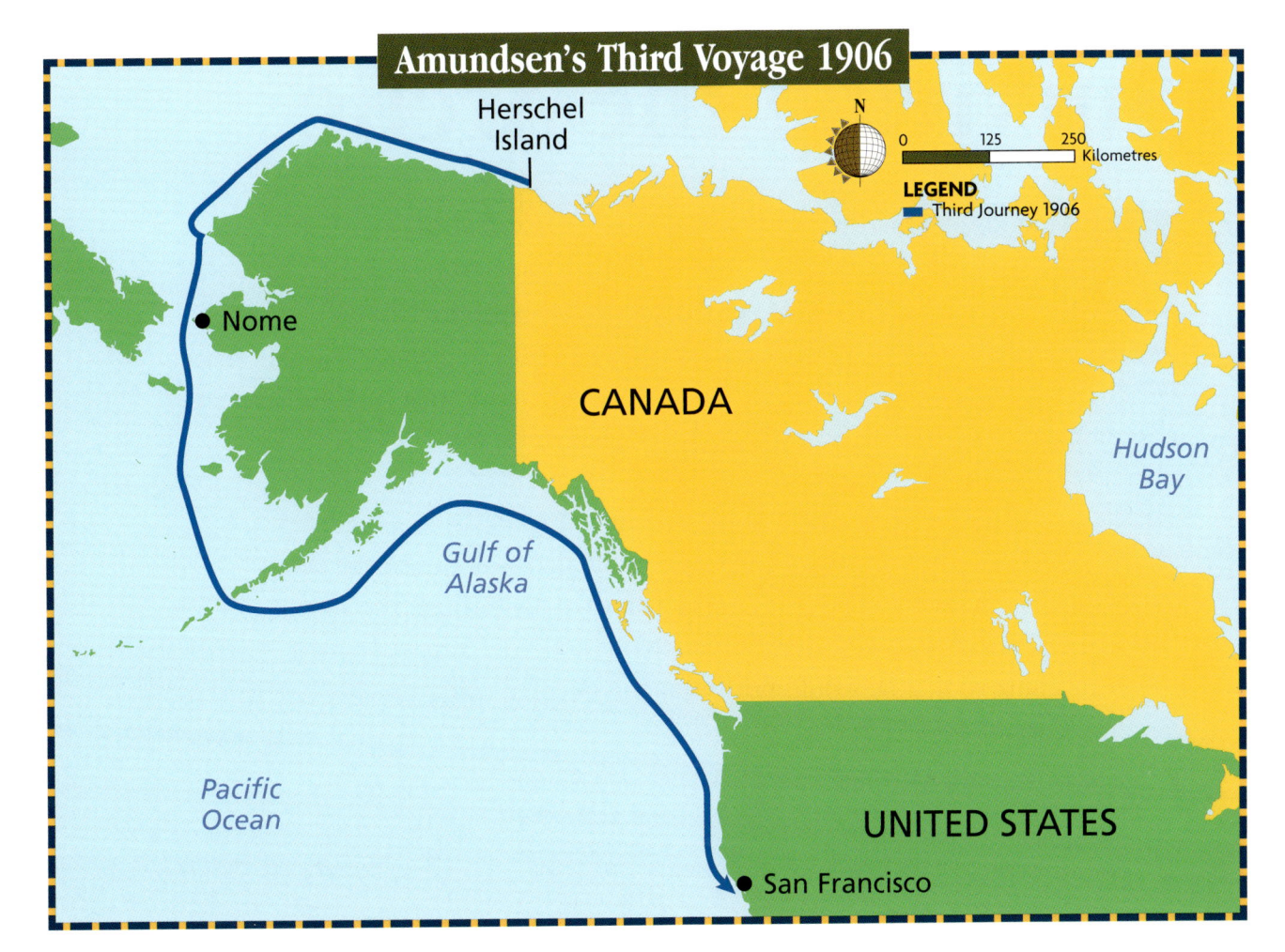

On the last day of August, the *Gjøa* reached Nome, Alaska. Amundsen and the crew stopped briefly to rest and celebrate their crossing of the Northwest Passage. Then, they continued on to San Francisco, California. Arriving on October 19, Amundsen and his crew were met by cheering crowds. Their journey through the Northwest Passage had made them international heroes.

Amundsen spent the next two years travelling the world. He gave many speeches about his journey through the Northwest Passage, his experiences living in the Arctic, the people he met, and his scientific findings. The tour helped him raise enough money to pay back everyone who had invested in his trip. It also made him very well known and respected.

Explorer Essentials

Amundsen donated the *Gjøa* to the people of San Francisco. The ship was put on display in Golden Gate Park until 1974. It was then returned to Oslo, and can be seen today in the Norwegian Maritime Museum.

Surviving the Arctic

Amundsen was fortunate to arrive home safely after his journey through the Northwest Passage. He had avoided much of the suffering regularly faced by polar explorers, such as extreme weather conditions, frostbite, **hypothermia**, illness, and starvation. Some of Amundsen's success was the result of help he received from a local Inuit group, the Netsiliks.

The Netsiliks showed Amundsen how to properly drive his sled dogs. They also showed him how to keep the runners on his sleds smooth so the sleds were easier for the dogs to pull and moved more easily through the snow. They taught him how to build wind-proof igloos and how to pace himself when travelling so that he would not sweat and become cold.

- The skills Amundsen learned from the Inuit helped him survive in the Arctic and made him one of the most successful polar explorers in history.

One of the most important things Amundsen learned from the Netsilik was how to make traditional Inuit clothing. Made of fur, the clothing was light, warm, and waterproof. Amundsen obtained some examples through trade and then made a complete collection of outfits. Typically, polar explorers wore wool clothing that was damp, heavy, and uncomfortable. Amundsen liked the loose fitting garments better. From then on, Amundsen wore Inuit-style fur clothing on his explorations.

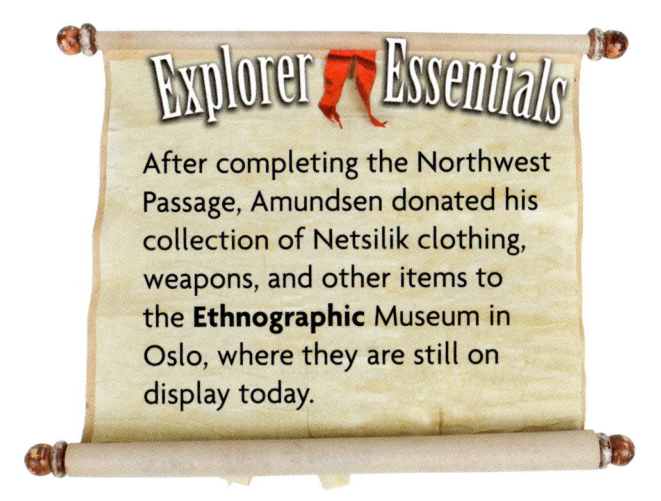

Explorer Essentials

After completing the Northwest Passage, Amundsen donated his collection of Netsilik clothing, weapons, and other items to the **Ethnographic** Museum in Oslo, where they are still on display today.

First-Hand Account

Amundsen described his encounters with the Netsilik in his autobiography. His description introduced the group to the rest of the world.

"The women are very adept at cutting out the black parts and the white parts of the caribou skins and fashioning them into beautiful shapes and then working these parts of the skins into elaborate patterns....Imagine, too, the interest I took in the implements used by these people. Their skill in taking the bones of freshly killed game and stretching and twisting them while still green into proper lengths and shapes from which to fashion spear heads and shaft needles for sewing, and other useful articles, was to me a fascinating example of human ingenuity."

Lasting Achievements and Legacies

Completing the Northwest Passage was a remarkable feat. In his early thirties, Amundsen had found what centuries of explorers had spent their lives seeking. Many people considered him a hero.

Amundsen returned to Norway with a wealth of valuable information about the Arctic. The scientific data he gathered during his two years at Gjøa Haven was extremely valuable. The amount of data and its level of detail provided experts with more than 20 years of study. Amundsen's descriptions and artifacts of Netsilik life were also important additions to the study of cultures.

- After returning from his voyage through the Northwest Passage, Amundsen began preparing for an expedition to be the first person to reach the North Pole. Amundsen did not succeed. He was beat by American Robert E. Peary.

Although completing the Northwest Passage had been his boyhood dream, Amundsen did not rest once he accomplished this goal. In 1911, he returned to Antarctica. Using the skills he had learned in Arctic Canada, on December 14, he became the first person to reach the South Pole. Later, in May 1926, Amundsen and two colleagues flew over the North Pole in an **airship**, called the *Norge*. They were the first people to fly over the North Pole and the first to fly from Europe to North America. Amundsen died two years later in May 1928, when he was 56 years old. He had been on his way to rescue a stranded colleague when his own plane crashed.

In September 2003, the 100th anniversary of Amundsen's voyage was celebrated at Gjøa Haven. A monument was built, and festivities took place, including an Inuit feast, traditional throat singing, and drum dancing.

- Roald Amundsen and his four-man team reached the South Pole, with the help of polar dogs, on December 14, 1911.

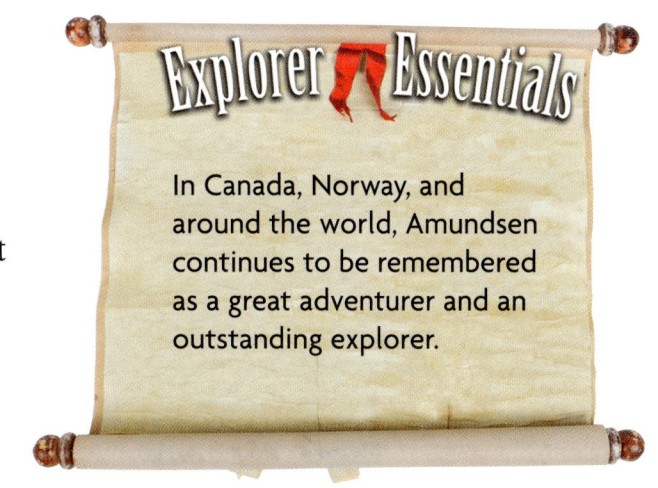

Explorer Essentials

In Canada, Norway, and around the world, Amundsen continues to be remembered as a great adventurer and an outstanding explorer.

Explorer Expeditions

Many explorers voyaged to Canada in search of riches and new land to claim on behalf of Europe.

Roald Amundsen

Roald Amundsen was a Norwegian explorer. In 1905, he became the first person to navigate the Northwest Passage. Six years later, he was the first person to the South Pole. He is considered one of the greatest polar explorers.

→ Amundsen 1903
→ Amundsen 1905-1906
→ Amundsen 1906

David Thompson

David Thompson was born in London, Great Britain. Throughout his lifetime, he became a very skilled mapmaker. He explored and mapped the fur-trading areas of western North America.

→ Thompson 1795
→ Thompson 1807
→ Thompson 1817-1827

Herschel Island
Banks Island
Great Bear Lake
Fort Franklin
Great Slave Lake
Fort Chipewyan
Lake Athabasca
Rocky Mountain House
Howse Pass
Kootenay Lake

UNITED STATES

26

John Franklin

John Franklin was a British explorer who sailed to numerous areas in the world, including Canada's Arctic region. Franklin died while trying to find the Northwest Passage, when his ships froze in the ice.

→ Franklin 1819
→ Franklin 1825
→ Franklin 1845

Pierre de La Vérendrye

Pierre de La Vérendrye was a farmer, soldier, and explorer, who was born in Canada. He travelled from eastern to western Canada in search of a western sea.

→ La Vérendrye 1731
→ La Vérendrye 1735
→ La Vérendrye 1738

Timeline

1872 Amundsen is born near Oslo, Norway.

1886 Amundsen's father dies.

1890 Amundsen completes school and joins the army.

1893 Amundsen's mother dies. He leaves medical school to become a polar explorer.

1897 Amundsen becomes first mate of the *Belgica* and travels to Antarctica.

1898 In February, the *Belgica* becomes frozen in sea ice. Amundsen is one of the first people to survive an Antarctic winter.

1899 The *Belgica* returns to Norway in March.

1900 Amundsen obtains his ship captain's license and purchases the *Gjøa*.

1903 Amundsen and his crew depart from Norway on June 16 in search of the Northwest Passage. They reach Gjøa Haven in September and are visited by the Netsilik in October.

1904 Amundsen proves that the North Magnetic Pole moves on April 26.

1905 Amundsen leaves Gjøa Haven on August 13. He meets the *Charles Hansson* on August 26, proving he has completed the Northwest Passage. He arrives in Eagle City on December 5, announcing his victory to the world.

1906 Amundsen returns to the *Gjøa* on March 12. Free from the ice, the *Gjøa* arrives in Nome, Alaska, in August. On October 19, Amundsen is welcomed as a hero in San Francisco.

1911 On December 14, Amundsen becomes the first person to reach the South Pole.

1926 Amundsen flies over the North Pole in an airship.

1928 Amundsen dies in the Arctic after his plane crashes on a rescue mission.

- Amundsen's ship the *Maud* was escorted home in 1926 after being lost at sea for two years.

Create a Compass

Earth is like a large magnet. It has two magnetic poles. The North Magnetic Pole is in the Canadian Arctic, and the South Magnetic Pole is off the coast of Antarctica. The needle of every compass points toward the North Magnetic Pole. This helps travellers find their way to a destination. You can make your own compass with a simple magnet and a CD or DVD.

Materials
a blank or old CD or DVD
a small magnet
a bowl, wide enough to hold the CD
glue
water

Instructions
1. Find the North Pole of your magnet.
2. Align the magnet parallel to the CD, so a pole is facing outward, toward the CD's edge.
3. Glue the magnet about 5 centimetres from the CD's outer edge. Adjust the distance depending on the size and weight of your magnet. Remember that if the magnet is too close to the edge, it will tip the CD. If the magnet is too close to the centre, it will weigh down your compass, preventing it from spinning.
4. Fill the bowl with water.
5. Lay the CD in the water, with the magnet side up.
6. Watch the magnet align itself in the direction of the Magnetic North Pole. Now, you have made a compass!

Quiz

1. Where and when was Amundsen born?

2. Who was Amundsen's boyhood hero?

3. On what ship did Amundsen serve as first mate?

4. Who was the first person to locate the North Magnetic Pole?

5. When did Amundsen and his crew leave Norway to begin their expedition to find the Northwest Passage?

6. What was the name of Amundsen's base camp on King William Island?

7. On what day did Amundsen and the crew meet the *Charles Hansson*?

8. Where did Amundsen finish his voyage?

9. What was the name of the Inuit group that helped Amundsen?

10. What did Amundsen do on December 14, 1911?

Answers
1. in Borge, near Oslo, Norway, in 1872
2. Sir John Franklin
3. the *Belgica*
4. James Clark Ross
5. at midnight on June 16, 1903
6. Gjøa Haven
7. August 26, 1905
8. in San Francisco
9. the Netsiliks
10. reached the South Pole

Websites

For more information about Amundsen and other Northwest Passage explorers, visit the following websites.

NOVA: Arctic Passage
Relive the expeditions of Franklin and Amundsen through journal entries, images, artifacts, and interactive quizzes.
www.pbs.org/wgbh/nova/arctic

Library and Archives Canada: Triumph in the High North
Read more about the adventures of Amundsen and other explorers in Canada.
www.collectionscanada.gc.ca/2/3/h3-1900-e.html

Books

Hern, Frances. *Arctic Explorers: In Search of the Northwest Passage*. Canmore: Altitude Publishing, 2007.

Karner, Julie. *Roald Amundsen: The Conquest of the South Pole.* New York: Crabtree Publishing, 2006.

Thompson, Gare. *Roald Amundsen and Robert Scott Race to the South Pole*. Des Moines: National Geographic Children's Books, 2007.

Glossary

airship: a craft that is lighter than air, can be steered, and usually has an engine
appendicitis: an infection in the appendix
Bering Strait: a waterway between Russia and Alaska, which connects the Arctic and Pacific Oceans
bow: the forward end of a ship
cairn: a mound of stones used to mark a location
creditors: a person to whom a debt is owed
ethnographic: a branch of science that deals with the description of individual cultures
first mate: the person who is second in command of a ship, after the captain
geomagnetism: the natural magnetic properties of Earth
hull: the frame or body of a ship
hypothermia: a dangerous condition of very low body temperature
Lancaster Sound: a body of water between Devon Island and Baffin Island in Nunavut
manoeuverability: capable of quickly and easily changing position
meteorology: a science that studies Earth's weather and atmosphere
pemmican: a mixture made of dried, pounded meat, melted fat, and berries
scurvy: a painful illness caused by a lack of vitamin C
sealing: the seal hunt
truculent: fierce, cruel, or savagely brutal

Index

Alaska 19, 20, 21, 28
Antarctica 8, 9, 25, 28, 29
Arctic 4, 5, 6, 7, 9, 10, 11, 12, 13, 14, 16, 19, 20, 21, 22, 24, 25, 27, 28, 29, 31

Belgica 8, 28, 30

Charles Hansson 18, 28, 30
clothing 14, 23
crew 5, 7, 8, 13, 14, 15, 16, 17, 18, 19, 20, 21, 28, 30

food 8, 15, 16
Franklin, Sir John 5, 6, 7, 10, 16, 27, 30, 31

Gjøa 12, 13, 14, 15, 16, 18, 19, 20, 21, 28
Gjøa Haven 16, 17, 18, 19, 24, 25, 28, 30
Greenland 16, 17

Inuit 16, 17, 18, 22, 23, 25, 30

Norge 25
North Magnetic Pole 11, 12, 16, 17, 28, 29, 30
North Pole 11, 24, 25, 28, 29
Northwest Passage 5, 6, 7, 10, 11, 12, 13, 15, 18, 19, 21, 22, 23, 24, 25, 26, 27, 28, 30, 31

Oslo, Norway 6, 7, 14, 21, 23, 28, 30

Ross, James Clark 11, 17, 30

San Francisco 20, 21, 28, 30
South Pole 25, 26, 28, 30, 31
supplies 13, 14, 15, 16